Table of Contents

THE MICROWAVE MAGIC

Microwave cooking is a healthy, quick, and easy way to make nutritious and delicious meals.

Microwave recipes are great for people on the go, people who live by themselves or just want an easy way to prepare food at home

We all know microwave ovens are convenient for reheating meals and coffee. But they can do so much more.

The microwave oven is also great for steaming vegetables, precooking and par-cooking some items like potatoes, steaming rice, and more etc.

WHY MICROWAVE RECIPES?

It is perfect for weeknight meals, the time and effort savings are undeniable. From prep, to cook, to clean up.

Cook and serve your steamed vegetables in the same bowl. Then pop it in the dishwasher. No need to dirty a pot or pan.

The microwave is also your friend on hot days when you don't want a hot kitchen.

Trust us, nobody will know if you follow our easy and delicious microwave recipes below.

THE FAIL-PROOF METHOD

Most vegetables have a high water content. And for that reason, microwave cooking and vegetables are bosom buddies.

This cooking method produces a quality likened to traditional steaming.

Bonus: microwave vegetable recipes often preserve more nutrients than other cooking techniques.

Also, unlike most other techniques, there's no fat needed during cooking.

RULES FOR A PERFECT RESULT

- POWER LEVEL + TIMING

Successful microwave cooking is all about balancing power and time.

You've likely experienced an over-microwaved morsel of food-turned-rubber at some point.

It's easy to overcook foods if microwaved too long with too much power.

SO start at 1 minute, then add 30-second intervals until your food is warmed through. Without being further cooked.

- COOK TIME

Microwave oven power output varies greatly. So cook time is approximate in all microwave recipes.

A good rule of thumb: when reaching the minimum cook time in a recipe, check your veggies in 30-second intervals.

Cook time can be added to under-cooked food. But once overcooked, you're done.

- Stirring the food at the mid-way point ensures even cooking.
- A tight-fitting plate over your bowl when directed is key. This method retains moisture to prevent food from drying out.
- Leaving microwave recipes covered for a minute post cook time adds more cook/steam time.

- KEEP IT SAFE.

When removing cooking vessels from the microwave, they often become hot.

"ALWAYS USE CAUTION AND REMOVE WITH HOT PADS OR GLOVES."

Also, use caution when removing plates from bowls as steam is deceptively hot and can burn you.

To avoid escaping steam, lift from the side and away from you.

- STEER CLEAR OF PLASTIC AND METAL.

Choose microwave and oven-safe vessels. Use a tight-fitting microwave-safe plate for the lid.

Even though some plastic states it is microwave safe, it's not. Plastic is known to leach into foods when heated. This includes plastic wrap and dishes.

Always avoid metal and metal trimmed dishes. They are not microwave-oven safe.

QUICK FIX MICROWAVE RECIPES

MICROWAVE CORN ON THE COB

INGREDIENTS;

- Corn on the Cob
- Butter
- Salt
- Pepper

INSTRUCTIONS

I. Pull off the silks at the top of the cob if they are soggy or falling off

II. Cook on full power for four minutes, or four and half minutes for two or three ears, and five for four ears, rotating halfway through

III. Carefully remove the cobs with kitchen tongs or a thick hot pad that to protect you from any hot moisture released by the corn

IV. Using a large kitchen knife, cut through the ear at its thickest point, cutting through the kernels, not just the stem to ensure it will slip off

V. Wrap the corn in a towel and squeeze the corn out of the hole made when you cut off

the stump. Just three or four squeezes should do the trick
VI. Remove any final silks and serve with butter and salt and pepper
VII. Shuck the corn
VIII. Wrap corn cob in a wet, not damp, paper towel
IX. Cook in microwave on full power for four minutes for one, four and half minutes for two or three, and five minutes with a rotation halfway through cooking.
X. Remove from microwave carefully with either tongs or thick hot pad
XI. Carefully unwarp each cob, and serve with butter and salt and pepper

PERFECTLY COOKED BROCCOLI

INGREDIENTS:

- 1-2 broccoli bunches (1½ pounds). Can substitute pre-cut broccoli florets.
- 1/3 cup water
- Sea salt, to taste
- Freshly ground black pepper, to taste

- 2 tablespoons garlic herb compound butter (optional)
- Lemon juice (optional)
- Lemon zest (optional)
- Red pepper flakes (optional)
- Grated Parmesan cheese (optional)

INSTRUCTIONS

I. Position the head of broccoli upside down on the cutting board. Hold the stem end at an angle. Cut off the florets. Slice larger florets in half.

II. With a vegetable peeler or a knife, remove any tough or dry areas along the stalk. Cut the stem into ¼" rounds. Note: For a very tender stalk, peel or cut away the outer layer (approximately 1/8 inch) before slicing the stem into rounds.

III. Place the broccoli florets and the water in a large microwave-safe bowl.

IV. Cover the bowl with a large microwave-safe dinner plate. Ensure the plate completely covers the bowl and fits snuggly. Microwave on high for 5 minutes.

V.   Using potholders, carefully remove the bowl and plate from the microwave. Keep the bowl covered for an additional minute.

VI.   Drain the broccoli in a colander set in the sink. Place compound butter in the bottom of the bowl used to cook the broccoli.

VII. After draining, place the broccoli back in the bowl. Stir to combine. Alternately melt the butter in a small microwave-safe bowl in 15-second intervals at 30% power until it melts. Toss the broccoli with the melted butter and serve.

MELTING MUSHROOMS

INGREDIENTS:

- 1 pound of Cremini Mushrooms
- 1-2 tablespoons extra-virgin olive oil or, for additional flavor, use our Garlic Herb Compound Butter
- Sea salt, to taste
- Freshly ground black pepper, to taste

INSTRUCTIONS

I.   Wash the mushrooms just before ready to use. Place on a paper towel to dry. Alternately, wipe mushrooms with a damp paper towel to remove dirt and debris.

II.   Slice into ¼ inch slices.

III.   Place the mushroom slices in a microwave oven-safe bowl. Cover with a large dinner plate that fits snugly over the bowl. Microwave on high for 4 minutes. With hot pads, remove the mushrooms from the microwave oven and stir.

IV.   Cook in additional 30-second increments until mushrooms have released liquid and are tender.

V.   Drain the mushrooms in a large strainer over a bowl if you would like to save the liquid for another use.

VI.   Drizzle the mushrooms with olive oil, salt, and pepper. Or a add a simple compound butter like our Garlic Herb Butter. Stir to combine.

MICROWAVE HOMEMADE MAC & CHEESE

INGREDIENTS:

- 16-ounce package of pasta, small shells or elbow macaroni
- 2 cups milk
- 6 tablespoons flour
- 1 teaspoon salt
- ¼ teaspoon pepper
- Two pinches nutmeg (optional)
- 2 cups shredded cheese
- ½ cup Panko bread crumbs (optional)
- 1 tablespoon melted butter (optional)

INSTRUCTIONS

I.   Put the water for the pasta on to boil.
II. Shred cheese. In a good-sized microwave-safe bowl, whisk together well the milk, flour, salt, pepper and nutmeg (if using). Stir in the cheese.
III. When water comes to a boil, add pasta and cook according to package directions.
IV. While pasta is cooking, cook the milk-cheese mixture in the microwave on full

power 1-2 minutes at a time, whisking after each time. Keep cooking until cheese is fully melted and you have a nice, smooth sauce (probably about 5 minutes total).

V. Drain pasta, return to pot then add sauce and mix well.

VI. If you want to top the mac & cheese with breadcrumbs, boil the pasta in a wide, oven-safe pot. After the mac & cheese is all mixed together in the pot, sprinkle evenly with panko bread crumbs (about ½ cup or so) then drizzle with butter. Place pan in oven under high broiler and cook until breadcrumbs start to brown, a few minutes. If you don't have an oven safe pot, feel free to transfer the mac & cheese to a 9" x 13" casserole dish before adding the bread crumbs and broiling in the oven.

MICROWAVE PROTEIN WHEY CAKE

INGREDIENTS:

- 1 Packet Sweetener
- 1 Tablespoon Cocoa Powder
- 1 ½ Scoops Protein Powder - Your choice flavor
- 1 Teaspoon Ground Cinnamon
- 1 ¼ Servings Pancake Mix
- 3-4 Ounces Water
- 6 Tablespoons Whipped Topping - Fat Free

INSTRUCTIONS

I. Take out a bowl and mix all of your ingredients together aside from your Whipped Topping

II. Coat a microwave safe bowl with non-stick cooking spray

III. Pour your mixed ingredients in

IV. Microwave for 1-2 minutes depending on how powerful your microwave is

V. Top with your Whipped Topping and/or anything else you want like Peanut Butter and Chocolate Chips!

BEEF & BROCCOLI

INGREDIENTS:

- 1½–2 lb./680 g–1 kg flank steak, cut into 4 quarters
- 1 tsp. of Steak Seasoning
- 4 garlic cloves, peeled and minced
- 1¾ cups beef stock, divided
- ½ cup low-sodium soy sauce
- 1 tbsp. sesame oil
- ¼ cup brown sugar
- 3 tbsp. corn starch
- 14-oz./415 g bag frozen broccoli florets

INSTRUCTIONS

I. Season steak with seasoning and place in base of Microwave Pressure Cooker.

II. In a medium bowl, combine garlic, 1½ cups beef stock, soy sauce, sesame oil and brown sugar. Pour over steak. Add extra stock if meat is not fully submerged. Seal and microwave on high power 30 minutes.

III. Remove from microwave and allow pressure to release naturally until red pressure indicator fully lowers, about 10–15 minutes. Remove steak to a cutting board and pull apart using 2 forks.

IV. In small bowl, whisk together corn starch and remaining ¼ cup beef stock. Whisk into warm liquid in base of Pressure Cooker.

V. Stir frozen broccoli into liquid in Pressure Cooker. Seal and microwave on high power 5 minutes.

VI. Serve warm and over rice, if desired.

CHEESY VEGETABLE QUICHE WITH CAULIFLOWER CRUST

INGREDIENTS:

CAULIFLOWER CRUST

- 1 medium head of cauliflower
- ½ cup (45g) grated Parmesan cheese
- 1 large egg
- ½ teaspoon dried oregano
- ¼ teaspoon garlic powder
- ¼ teaspoon salt
- ¼ teaspoon black pepper

FILLING

- 1 10-ounce package (283g) frozen chopped spinach thawed and drained
- 1 large bell pepper chopped
- ½ of a yellow onion chopped; about ⅓ cup
- 2 cloves garlic chopped
- 4 large eggs
- 2 large egg whites
- 1 cup (240g) milk any
- ½ teaspoon salt
- ¼ teaspoon black pepper
- 4 ounces (114g) shredded cheese

INSTRUCTIONS

CAULIFLOWER CRUST

I. Preheat the oven to 450ºF (232ºC). Spray an 8" or 9" pie dish with non-stick spray and set aside.

II. Cut cauliflower into pieces, removing as much stem as possible and keeping the florets. Rinse the florets in a colander, place in a food processor, and pulse florets until they resemble corn meal.

III. Place processed cauliflower in a medium size microwave safe bowl and cook in the microwave on high for 5 minutes. Remove from microwave, set aside, and allow to cool for 10 minutes.

IV. After cauliflower has cooled, use a strong kitchen towel to wring out all of the moisture. Transfer dry cauliflower back to bowl.

V. In a small bowl, blend together Parmesan cheese, egg, and spices. Add to cooled cauliflower and mix together with a spatula or your hands.

VI. Transfer cauliflower to pie dish, smoothing it out with your hands, making sure to spread it evenly to cover the bottom and the sides of the dish.

VII. Bake crust for 15-20 minutes until edges are brown and overall crust starts browning. Allow to cool on wire rack while you prepare the filling.

FILLING

I. Decrease the oven to 350ºF (177ºC). Blot or squeeze out as much moisture as you can from your thawed spinach. If you heated your spinach to thaw it, make sure it is cool enough to handle. Put dry spinach in a large bowl and set aside.

II. Spray a large skillet with non-stick spray and heat over medium-high heat. Add bell pepper, onion, and garlic and season with a pinch of salt and black pepper. Cook mixture for 5-6 minutes, stirring frequently, or until tender. Spoon the cooked vegetables into the bowl with the spinach. Stir to combine and allow to cool.

III. In a medium size bowl, preferably with a spout, whisk the eggs, egg whites, milk, salt, and pepper until thoroughly combined. Set aside.

IV. Spoon spinach and vegetable mixture into cauliflower crust, top with shredded cheese, and pour the egg mixture evenly on top of cheese layer. Place a pie shield or foil around the exposed crust to prevent from burning.

V. Bake quiche for 40-42 minutes or until filling is set. Cool for 10 minutes on a wire rack before serving. Cover tightly and store in the refrigerator up to 4 days, or in the freezer up to 2 months. Thaw in refrigerator overnight and bake at 350°F (177ºC) until warmed through, about 25 minutes.

CREAMY CHICKEN ALFREDO IN A MUG

INGREDIENTS:

- 320g fresh fettuccine
- 330ml (11 /3 cups) Massel Chicken Style Liquid Stock
- 250ml (1 cup) thickened cream
- 2 tsp Dijon mustard
- 3 green shallots, thinly sliced
- 100g shredded barbecued chicken
- 40g butter, cut into cubes

INSTRUCTIONS

I. Divide the pasta among four 375ml (11 /2 cup) microwave-safe mugs. Pour over the chicken stock. Cover with plastic wrap. Microwave all 4 mugs on High for 8 minutes or until the stock has absorbed.

II. Meanwhile, whisk cream and mustard together in a jug.

III. Carefully uncover mugs. Divide shallot, chicken and butter among the mugs. Pour over cream mixture. Cover and microwave on High for 3 minutes or until heated through. Uncover and stir. Season with pepper to serve.

MICROWAVE SALMON

INGREDIENTS:

- 1 – single portion salmon filet
- salt and pepper
- 2 tablespoons mayonnaise
- 1-2 tablespoons sriracha sauce
- 2-3 fresh cut lemon slices
- 1 tablespoon parsley

INSTRUCTIONS

I. Rinse salmon filet with cold water and pat dry. Place the salmon skin side down in a microwave save container. Season the salmon with salt and pepper. Set aside. In a small bowl, combine mayonnaise and sriracha sauce. Generously spread the mayonnaise mixture on top of the fillet. Add lemon slices and parsley. Cover the dish tightly with microwave safe plastic wrap. Microwave the fish for 3.5 minutes. Check the center of the filet for doneness with a fork. If there is any uncooked fish, microwave for another 30-45 seconds. Garnish with additional parsley and lemon wedges.

MICROWAVE RASPBERRY JAM

INGREDIENTS:

- 250g fresh raspberries
- 1 cup caster sugar
- 1 tbsp lemon juice

INSTRUCTIONS

I. Combine raspberries, caster sugar and lemon juice in a microwave-safe bowl. Cook on High, stirring every 1-2 minutes (stir more often at end of cooking) for 10 minutes or until thickened. To test if jam is ready, place 1 tsp jam on a chilled saucer.

II. Place in freezer for 1-2 minutes or until cooled slightly. Lightly push jam with your finger. If surface wrinkles, it's ready. Transfer to a sterilised jar.

MICROWAVE RICE PUDDING IN A MUG

INGREDIENTS:

- 250ml (1 cup) milk
- 1 egg
- 2 tbsp caster sugar
- Pinch salt
- 1 tsp vanilla extract
- 1/4 tsp ground cinnamon
- 2 x 125g tubs microwave long-grain white rice
- Ground cinnamon, extra, to dust

INSTRUCTIONS

I. Place milk, egg, sugar, salt, vanilla and cinnamon in a bowl and whisk to combine.
II. Divide milk mixture between 2 x 350ml microwave-safe mugs. Using a fork, separate rice in one tub. Add to one mug. Repeat with remaining rice and mug.
III. Microwave one mug on 30% power for 6 minutes or until mixture thickens and rice

pudding is set. Repeat with remaining mug. Stand for 2 minutes before serving dusted with a little extra cinnamon.

MICROWAVE CINNAMON MAPLE QUINOA BREAKFAST BOWL

INGREDIENTS:

- 1/2 cup quinoa
- 1 cup cold water
- 1/2 teaspoon cinnamon + more for garnish
- 2 teaspoons butter
- milk or cream, to taste
- maple syrup to taste
- banana slices

INSTRUCTIONS

I. Place quinoa in water and rinse well.
II. Drain quinoa, then stir in 1 cup cold water, 1/2 teaspoon cinnamon and 1 teaspoon butter.
III. Microwave on high for 4 minutes. Stir and microwave 3 more minutes. Remove from microwave,

IV. cover with foil and sit 2 minutes. Fluff quinoa and stir in remaining butter. Divide between 2 bowls and top with milk, maple syrup, banana slices and cinnamon to taste.

MICROWAVE BREAD AND BUTTER PUDDING

INGREDIENTS:

- 5 slices spicy fruit bread
- 50g butter, softened
- 1/4 cup dried figs, quartered
- 2 egg yolks
- 4 eggs
- 1 cup milk
- 1/2 cup caster sugar
- 1 tsp vanilla extract
- Icing sugar mixture, to serve

INSTRUCTIONS

I. Spread both sides of bread with butter. Cut into quarters to make triangles. Arrange bread triangles, slightly overlapping, in a 5 cup-capacity, 16cm x 25cm heatproof, microwave-safe dish. Sprinkle with figs.

II. Whisk egg yolks, eggs, milk, sugar and vanilla together in a large jug. Pour egg mixture over bread. Press bread down gently into egg mixture. Set aside for 10 minutes to allow egg mixture to be absorbed.

III. Microwave, uncovered, on MEDIUM (50%) for 10 minutes or until egg mixture has just set.

IV. Meanwhile, preheat grill on medium. Place bread and butter pudding under grill. Grill for 5 minutes or until top is golden. Serve dusted with icing sugar.

MICROWAVE TOASTED NUTS

INGREDIENTS:

- Almonds (sliced): 7-10 minutes
- Almonds (whole): 10 minutes
- Chestnuts: 25 minutes
- Hazelnuts: 12-15 minutes
- Macadamia Nuts: 12-15 minutes
- Pecans: 10-15 minutes
- Pine Nuts: 5 minutes
- Walnuts: 10-15 minutes

- Peanuts (in shell): 15-20 minutes
- Peanuts (shelled): 20-25 minutes

INSTRUCTIONS

I.   Spread a single layer of nuts on a microwave safe plate.

II. Cook them in 1 minute intervals on full power, until the nuts have a crisp crunch and toasted flavor and have become fragrant. The amount of time it takes varies per nut. You will not get the same dark color you get from oven or pan toasting, but this will do in a hurry when you don't want to dirty a pan or heat up the oven for such a simple task.

SKINNING NUTS:

If you have toasted any nuts that have skins on them, like peanuts or hazelnuts, simply allow them to cool for a few minutes, and then place the nuts in a clean and dry kitchen towel.

Rub them vigorously with the towel, and the skins will slip right off. Don't worry about any skins that do remain, however. They will not affect any food you add them to, and the skins are safe to eat.

MICROWAVE SCRAMBLED EGGS

INGREDIENTS:

- 2 eggs

INSTRUCTIONS

I. Break eggs into container. Add 2 tablespoons cold water. Whisk to combine. Cover with lid. Open vent.

II. Microwave on high (100%) for 30 seconds. Stir with a fork. Microwave, covered, for 30 seconds. Stir. Microwave, covered, for 10 seconds or until almost set. Close vent. Stand for 1 minute. Serve with muffin and smoked salmon.

CLASSY FRENCH TOAST CASSEROLE IN A MUG

INGREDIENTS:

- 1 tablespoon butter
- 1 egg
- 3 tablespoons milk
- Dash cinnamon
- 2 slices your favorite bread

INSTRUCTIONS

I. Cut bread into bite size pieces.
II. Melt butter in a microwave safe mug.
III. Add egg, milk, and cinnamon to melted butter and mix together.
IV. Add bread to mixture and stir together until all of the bread cubes are completely coated.
V. Microwave for 2 minutes. Add syrup if desired and enjoy!

MICROWAVE PEANUT BUTTER AND BANANA OATMEAL

INGREDIENTS:

- 1/2 cup rolled oats
- 1 cup milk your choice
- 2 tablespoons peanut butter
- Cinnamon to taste
- 1 banana

INSTRUCTIONS

I.   Combine milk, cinnamon, and rolled oats in a microwave safe bowl and cook for 2 minutes. While oatmeal is cooking, slice banana.

II.   Stir in peanut butter and cook for an additional minute or until oats are soft.

III.   Top with a banana and any additional peanut butter you desire. Enjoy!

MICROWAVE BEEF STROGANOFF

INGREDIENTS:

- 1 tbsp olive oil
- 1 onion, finely chopped
- 2 tbsp tomato paste
- 1/2 cup plain flour
- 1 1/2 tbsp paprika
- 1kg beef rump steak, cut into strips
- 420g can cream of mushroom soup
- 1 1/2 cups Massel beef stock
- 2 tbsp tomato sauce
- 1 tbsp Worcestershire sauce
- 100g mushrooms, thinly sliced

- 1/2 cup sour cream
- 1/3 cup flat-leaf parsley leaves, chopped
- steamed rice, to serve

INSTRUCTIONS

I. Place oil and onion into a 2-litre capacity dish. Microwave, uncovered, for 2 minutes on HIGH (100%) power. Add tomato paste. Cook a further 1 minute on HIGH.

II. Combine flour, paprika, salt and pepper. Add beef. Toss. Add to onion mixture. Stir in soup, stock and sauces. Microwave, covered, for 1 hour on DEFROST-MEDIUM LOW (30%) power, stirring every 10 minutes.

III. Add mushrooms and sour cream. Microwave 10 minutes on same power. Sprinkle with parsley. Serve with rice.

MICROWAVE EGG, CANADIAN BACON & CHEESE MUFFIN

INGREDIENTS:

- large EGG, beaten 1

- Canadian bacon OR thin slice deli ham 1 slice
- shredded cheddar cheese 1 Tbsp.
- wheat English muffin, split, toasted

INSTRUCTIONS

I. LINE the bottom of 8-oz. microwave-safe ramekin or custard cup with Canadian bacon. (If using ham it may be necessary to fold the slice in half.) POUR egg over Canadian bacon.

II. Microwave on high 30 seconds; STIR. Microwave until egg is almost set, 15 to 30 seconds longer. SEASON with salt and pepper if desired.

III. TOP with cheese. SERVE immediately on English muffin.

SPICY PUMPKIN MICROWAVE RISOTTO

INGREDIENTS:

- 1 litre Massel chicken style liquid stock
- 2 tbsp olive oil

- 1 small red onion, finely chopped
- 2 garlic cloves, crushed
- 1 1/2 tsp ground coriander
- 1 1/2 tsp ground cumin
- 1/2 tsp dried chilli flakes
- 750g butternut pumpkin, peeled, cut into 2cm pieces
- 1 tbsp honey
- 2 cups arborio rice
- 1 cup boiling water
- 1/3 cup toasted pine nuts
- Fresh coriander leaves, to serve

INSTRUCTIONS

I. Place stock in a microwave-safe jug. Microwave on high (100%) for 2 minutes or until hot. Cover to keep warm.

II. Combine oil, onion, garlic , ground coriander, cumin and chilli in a 2 litre-capacity microwave-safe dish (with lid). Microwave on high (100%) for 2 minutes or until onion has softened. Add pumpkin and honey. Microwave, covered, on high (100%)

for 2 minutes or until pumpkin has just softened.

III. Add rice. Stir to combine. Microwave on high (100%) for 1 minute. Add 3 cups stock. Stir to combine. Microwave, covered, on high (100%) for 10 minutes or until liquid has reduced by half.

IV. Add boiling water and remaining stock. Stir to combine. Microwave, covered, on medium (50%), for 5 minutes. Stir. Microwave, covered, on medium (50%) for 5 minutes or until almost all liquid has absorbed.

V. Stand, covered, for 5 minutes or until liquid has completely absorbed. Stir in pine nuts. Serve topped with coriander.

MEXICAN-STYLE STUFFED HOT POTATOES

INGREDIENTS:

- 4 (about 200g each) coliban potatoes, unpeeled
- 80ml (1/3 cup) taco sauce
- 90g (1/3 cup) light sour cream

- 1 avocado, halved, stone removed and coarsely chopped

INSTRUCTIONS

I. Line a microwave-safe plate with paper towel. Use a fork to prick the coliban potatoes, unpeeled, all over. Place potatoes on the lined plate. Cook in microwave on High/800watts/ 100% for 15 minutes or until tender. Set aside for 3 minutes or until cool enough to handle.

II. Use a sharp knife to cut the top off each potato. Discard the tops. Divide taco sauce, light sour cream and avocado among the potatoes. Season with pepper to serve.

TIKKA CHICKEN & BEAN CURRY WITH PAPPADUMS

INGREDIENTS:

- 8 mini pappadums
- 300g (1 1/2 cups) Basmati rice
- 1 tbsp olive oil
- 1 brown onion, coarsely chopped

- 65g (1/4 cup) Patak's Tikka Masala curry paste
- 12 fresh curry leaves
- 1 x 400ml can coconut cream
- 6 (about 660g) chicken thigh fillets, cut into 4cm pieces
- 200g green beans, topped, cut into 5cm lengths
- 2 tomatoes, coarsely chopped
- Fresh coriander leaves, to serve
- Natural yoghurt, to serve

INSTRUCTIONS

I. Place half the pappadums on a microwave-safe plate lined with non-stick baking paper. Cook, turning once, on high/800watts/100%, for 1-2 minutes or until puffed and golden. Repeat with remaining pappadums.

II. Place the rice in a microwave-safe bowl. Add enough water to cover the rice by 2cm. Cover with a lid or 2 layers of plastic wrap. Place in microwave on a sheet of non-stick baking paper. Cook, covered, on High/800watts/100% for 5 minutes. Cook, covered, on Medium/ 500watts/50% for a further 7 minutes. Set aside, covered, for 5-10 minutes.

III. Meanwhile, place oil and onion in a 3L (12-cup) capacity microwave-safe bowl. Cook, uncovered, on High/800watts/100% for 3 minutes. Add the curry paste and curry leaves, and cook, uncovered, on high/800watts/100% for 30 seconds.

IV. Add the coconut cream and chicken to the onion mixture and stir until well combined. Cook, uncovered, stirring once, on Medium/500watts/50% for 10 minutes.

V. Stir in the beans and tomato. Cook, uncovered, on medium/500watts/50% for 5 minutes or until beans are bright green and tender crisp and chicken is cooked through. Cover and set aside for 5 minutes.

VI. Use a fork to separate rice grains. Divide the rice and curry among serving bowls. Top with coriander and serve with yoghurt and pappadums.

BLUEBERRY BANANA MICROWAVE BAKED OATS

INGREDIENTSL:

- 1/2 cup old-fashioned rolled oats
- 1 tablespoon ground flax seed
- 1 egg
- 1/2 cup unsweetened vanilla almond milk
- 1/3 banana, mashed
- 1/4 teaspoon cinnamon
- 2 teaspoons maple syrup
- 1/3 cup fresh blueberries

INSTRUCTIONS

I. Spray a medium to large microwave-safe mug or small bowl with cooking spray and inside combine all ingredients except blueberries. Then, stir in blueberries.

II. Microwave on high for 2-3 minutes.

III. Stir in extra milk, yogurt or nut butter; if desired.

JELLY DONUT IN A MUG

INGREDIENTS:

- 2 tablespoons (1oz/30g) Butter
- 4 tablespoons all-purpose flour
- 1 Egg yolk
- 2 tablespoons sugar
- 1 tablespoon milk
- 1/2 teaspoon baking powder
- 1/4 teaspoon ground cinnamon
- 1 tablespoon Strawberry jam
- Cinnamon sugar to garnish

INSTRUCTIONS

I. Place butter into a microwavable mug and microwave until just melted. (roughly 20 seconds)

II. Add in the remaining ingredients; mix well with a fork until just combined

III. Once the batter is mixed place the spoonful of jam down into the batter to get a jammy center

IV. Microwave for 45 seconds or until it is firm on top. (Cooking time is based on my

1200W microwave so your timing might vary) Always keep a close eye on your mug while in the microwave so it doesn't overflow or overcook.

V.   Sprinkle some cinnamon sugar on top and enjoy straight away!

MICROWAVE TOMATO, RICOTTA AND SPINACH RISOTTO

INGREDIENTS:

- 3 1/4 cups boiling water
- 2 Massel vegetable stock cubes, crumbled
- 2 tbsp tomato paste
- 2 tbsp olive oil
- 1 small brown onion, finely chopped
- 1 garlic clove, crushed
- 1/2 cup dry white wine
- 2 cups arborio rice
- 400g can crushed tomatoes
- 200g fresh ricotta cheese, crumbled
- 50g baby spinach
- 2/3 cup shredded fresh basil leaves

INSTRUCTIONS

I.   Place boiling water in a heatproof jug.
     Crumble over stock cubes. Stir to dissolve.
     Add tomato paste. Stir to combine. Cover to
     keep warm.

II. Combine oil, onion and garlic in a 2 litre-
     capacity, microwave-safe dish (with lid).
     Microwave on high (100%) for 2 minutes or
     until onion has softened. Stir in wine.
     Microwave on high (100%) for 1 minute or
     until wine is hot.

III. Add rice. Stir to combine. Microwave on
     high (100%) for 1 minute. Add 21/2 cups
     stock mixture. Stir to combine. Microwave,
     covered, on high (100%) for 10 minutes or
     until liquid has reduced by half.

IV. Add tomato and remaining stock mixture.
     Stir to combine. Microwave, covered, on
     medium (50%) for 5 minutes. Stir.
     Microwave, covered, on medium (50%) for
     4 minutes or until almost all liquid has
     absorbed.

V.   Stir in half the ricotta. Add spinach and
     shredded basil. Stir until spinach has just

wilted. Season with salt and pepper. Serve topped with basil leaves and remaining ricotta.

MICROWAVE CARAMEL SELF-SAUCING PUDDING

INGREDIENTS:

- 1 cup self-raising flour
- 1 1/4 cups firmly packed brown sugar
- 60g butter, melted, cooled
- 1/2 cup milk
- 1 egg
- 1/2 cup chopped pecan nuts
- 1 cup boiling water
- icing sugar mixture, to serve
- Ice-cream, to serve

INSTRUCTIONS

I. Grease a 6cm-deep, 6 cup-capacity, heatproof, microwave-safe dish.

II. Combine flour and 1/2 cup sugar in a bowl. Make a well in the centre. Add butter, milk and egg. Whisk to combine. Stir in pecans.

Spoon mixture into prepared dish. Smooth top.

III. Combine boiling water and remaining sugar in a heatproof jug. Stir until sugar has dissolved. Pour mixture over the back of a large metal spoon to evenly cover pudding batter.

IV. Place dish on a microwave-safe rack or upturned dinner plate. Cook, uncovered, on medium (50%), for 9 to 10 minutes or until a skewer inserted into the edge of the pudding comes out clean. Carefully remove from microwave. Stand for 1 minute. Dust with icing sugar. Serve with ice-cream.

WHITE CHOCOLATE TRUFFLES

INGREDIENTS:

- 60ml (1/4 cup) thickened cream
- 2 x 180g pkt good-quality white chocolate, finely chopped
- 2 tsp Malibu liqueur

INSTRUCTIONS

I. Place the cream and half the chocolate in a medium heatproof bowl and place over a medium saucepan half-filled with simmering water (make sure the bowl doesn't touch the water). Use a metal spoon to stir occasionally until chocolate melts and the mixture is smooth. Remove from heat and stir in liqueur. Cover with plastic wrap and place in the fridge for 1 hour or until firm enough to roll into balls.

MICROWAVE CHICKEN PIZZA & PIZZA SAUCE

INGREDIENTS:

- 6 English Muffins
- 1 pound of Chicken (boneless, boiled and chopped)
- 1 ¾ cups of Shredded Mozzarella Cheese
- Hot Pepper Flakes (to taste)
- ¾ cup of Pizza Sauce

INGREDIENTS OF PIZZA SAUCE:

- 3 large Yellow Onions (minced)

- 3 cloves of Garlic (Lasan) (minced)
- 2 quarts of (canned) or fresh Italian Tomatoes
- 1 (16 oz.) can of Tomato Puree
- 1 tsp. of Whole Oregano
- 1 tsp. of Whole Basil
- 1 tsp. of Salt
- 1/4 tsp. of Black Peppers
- 3 tbsp. of Butter
- 3 tbsp. of Olive Oil

INSTRUCTIONS

I. Split and lightly toast English muffins in toaster, when toasted, place on plate (microwave safe). Spoon spread pizza sauce onto each muffin, then adds chicken and shredded mozzarella cheese.

II. You can fit 4 split English muffins on plate at one time. Microwave on high until cheese bubbles (About 1 minute or so).

PIZZA SAUCES:

III. In a Dutch oven or large skillet, melt the butter with the olive oil and slowly but completely sauté the garlic and onion. Add the tomatoes, salt, black pepper, oregano, basil and puree. Bring to a boil, then simmer covered for two hours. Stir occasionally, crushing the tomatoes with a potato masher. Continue to mash, stir, and simmer partially covered until the sauce reaches the consistency of a rich soup. (If you find you have too many or too large tomato seeds left in the sauce, you may run the sauce through a sieve, (strainer). Set the sauce aside to cool or refrigerate before applying it to your pizza dough.)

OPEN-FACED BREAKFAST BURRITO PRINT

INGREDIENTS:

- 1 low-carb flour tortilla with 100 calories or less
- 1/2 cup (about 4 large) egg whites or fat-free liquid egg substitute
- 2 tbsp. black beans
- 2 tbsp. shredded reduced-fat Mexican blend cheese
- 1/8 tsp. garlic powder
- 1/8 tsp. onion powder

- 2 tbsp. salsa
- 2 tbsp. light sour cream
- 1 tbsp. chopped fresh cilantro
- Optional topping: sliced black olives

INSTRUCTIONS

I.   Place a tortilla in a wide microwave-safe mug or bowl, allowing it to naturally fold to fit the shape. Carefully pour egg whites/substitute into the center of the tortilla.
II. Add beans, cheese, garlic powder, and onion powder. Microwave for 2 minutes, or until set.
III. Top with salsa, sour cream, and cilantro.
IV. Eat it right out of the mug/bowl, or transfer it to a plate.

EASY MICROWAVE BREAKFAST BOWL

INGREDIENTS:

- 1 large potatoes, diced
- 2 tbsp carrots, diced
- 2 tbsp broccoli, sliced
- 2 tbsp bell peppers, sliced

- 2 eggs
- 1 tbsp milk
- 1 oz cheddar cheese, shredded
- Pinch of salt and pepper

INSTRUCTIONS

I. Dice potatoes and carrots. Smaller it is, faster it will cook in the microwave. Transfer into a microwave safe bowl and coat with salt, and pepper.

II. Place a wet paper towel on top of the potatoes. Microwave until inside is soft when you pierce with a fork. About 5-7 minutes. Caution: it is hot when you take out of the microwave!

III. Meanwhile, dice all the vegetables.

IV. Coat a microwave safe bowl or ramekin with cooking spray or butter. Add eggs, mushroom, carrots, milk, salt and pepper, and mix until well combined.

V. Microwave on high for 30 seconds. Take them out and mix. Repeat until eggs are fully cooked

VI.   Lay the scrambled eggs on top of cooked potatoes. Sprinkle cheese on top and microwave until the cheese is fully melted.

VII.   Sprinkle some chives or basil or any other herbs that you have in hand. Enjoy!

COOKIE DOUGH MICROWAVE OATMEAL

INGREDIENTS:

- 1/2 cup rolled oats
- 2/3 cup plain, unsweetened almond milk
- 1/2 tablespoon cashew butter any kind of nut butter will work
- 2 teaspoons maple syrup
- 1/2 tablespoon mini chocolate chips for topping

INSTRUCTIONS

I.   In a microwave safe bowl, mix togehter rolled oats, unsweetened almond milk, nut butter, and maple syrup.

II.   Place bowl in microwave and cook on high for 1 minute.

III.   Stir oatmeal and place back in microwave. Cook for another minute. Remove and stir again.

IV.   Let cool for 2 minutes before topping with chocolate chips.

EASY MICROWAVE BREAKFAST CASSEROLE

INGREDIENTS:

- 1 slice bread, cubed
- 1 large egg, beaten
- 3 tablespoons milk
- 1/4 cup cooked diced ham
- 1 dash Worcestershire sauce
- 2 tablespoons shredded cheddar cheese
- 1/4 teaspoon dry mustard
- 1/8 teaspoon salt
- 1 dash freshly ground black pepper

INSTRUCTIONS

I.   Combine all ingredients in a 6-inch microwave-safe serving bowl. Blend well. Cover tightly with plastic wrap, then poke a few small holes in the top to vent.

II. Cook on MEDIUM-HIGH, or 80 percent power, for 4 1/2 to 5 1/2 minutes. Halfway through cooking time, turn dish a half-turn. Let stand, covered, for 30 seconds to finish cooking.

MICROWAVE HOT DOGS

INGREDIENTS:

- 2 hot dogs of choice
- 2 hot dog buns
- 1 tablespoon cold water or broth

INSTRUCTIONS

I. Preheat or toast your buns using the microwave, oven or skillet. Keep warm.
II. Take two large sheets of paper towel and dampen with the cold water or broth.
III. Wrap the hot dogs loosely in the paper towel and place on a microwave-safe plate.
IV. Place in the microwave and close the door. Microwave on full power for 30 seconds (or 45 seconds for a small microwave or 20 seconds for a powerful microwave).

V.   Open the door and check if the hot dog is heated through, taking care as it may be hot.

VI.   Repeat in 20 second intervals until the hot dog is to your liking. Note: jumbo dogs will take considerably more time than standard size dogs.

VII. Place the hot dogs into the warm buns and add your favorite toppings.

**Adjust the times above up or down based on a weaker or stronger microwave oven.

MICROWAVE RICE

INGREDIENTS:

- 2 cups white rice, or jasmine rice or basmati rice
- 3 cups water, or broth

INSTRUCTIONS

I.   Add rice to a microwave-safe bowl or microwave rice cooker. Pour in enough water to cover easily.

II.   Swish the rice around with your fingertips and drain the water through a sieve. Repeat 2-3 times until the water is mostly clear.

III.   Add the correct amount of water for cooking and cover.

IV.   Microwave at 100% or High Power for 10 minutes (see note).

V.   When the cycle is complete, microwave at 50% or Medium Power for 2 more minutes.

VI.   Remove the rice from the microwave and let it rest covered and undisturbed for 3 minutes.

VII. Fluff with a fork and serve.

BANANA BREAD IN A MUG

INGREDIENTS:

- 1/4 cup mashed banana
- 6 tbsp spelt, white, or oat flour
- 1 tbsp sweetener of choice
- 1/2 tsp baking powder
- 1/4 tsp cinnamon
- 1/8 tsp salt
- 1 1/2 tbsp oil, butter, or additional banana
- optional 1-2 tbsp chocolate chips

INSTRUCTIONS

I.   Combine all ingredients in a greased mug or bowl. Bake either in the oven or microwave until fluffy and cake-like. (It takes around 60-90 seconds in the microwave, depending on wattage. Or bake at 350 F for about 14 minutes.)

MICROWAVE FUDGE

INGREDIENTS:

- 18 oz chocolate chips
- 2 TBS butter
- 1 14 oz can sweetened condensed milk

INSTRUCTIONS

II.   Put chocolate chips, butter, and sweetened condensed milk in a large microwave safe bowl.

III. Microwave for 2 minutes.

IV.   Stir everything together as much as you can.

V.   Microwave for additional 30 second increments until you can stir it completely together. (Maybe 1 more minute).

VI.   Pour chocolate into a lined 9x9 glass pan or into cookie cutters and spread evenly.

VII. Decorate with colorful candies or sprinkles if desired.

STRAWBERRY MOCHI

INGREDIENTS:

- 6 fresh strawberries (small and round strawberries)
- 1 cup red bean paste (you might need more or less depending on the size of your strawberries)
- 3/4 cup Mochiko (or Shiratamako Sweet rice flour)
- 4 tablespoons sugar
- 3/4 cup water
- 1/2 cup cornstarch for dusting

INSTRUCTIONS

I.   Rinse the strawberries and remove green leaves. Then dry them completely. (Make sure to dry them properly before covering them with the red bean paste.)

II.   Divide the red bean paste into 6 equal-sized balls. Flatten each ball and wrap each strawberry with the red bean paste. Set them aside.

III. In a microwave-safe bowl, whisk together mochiko, sugar, and water. It's important to whisk until everything is dissolved completely.

IV.   Cover the bowl with plastic wrap or kitchen towel loosely.

V.   Microwave at full power for 2 minutes. Take it out and mix with a wet spatula. Cover and microwave for 30 more seconds until the dough becomes slightly translucent.

VI.   Transfer the cooked mochi dough onto the cornstarch-dusted parchment paper. Sprinkle a thin layer of cornstarch onto the dough.

VII. Divide the dough into 6 equal parts and flatten each one into a circular shape. You can easily stretch the dough using your hands. (If your dough is too hot, wait for a few minutes until it's cool enough to handle. Don't wait too long or your dough won't be stretchy enough.)

VIII.   Place each red bean paste covered strawberry in the center of each mochi wrapper. Make sure the pointing end is positioned at the center of the wrapper.

IX.   Pinch the four corners of the mochi wrapper, and then pinch the remaining corners together.

X.   Tap the bottom of mochi with cornstarch. Brush the assembled green tea mochi with a brush gently to remove excess cornstarch.

XI.   Repeat this process for the rest of the dough and fillings. Serve at room temperate. They can be store in the fridge for up to 2 days.

CARROT CAKE MUG CAKE

INGREDIENTS:

Mug Cake

- 1/4 cup flour
- 2 tbsp brown sugar
- 1/4 tsp cinnamon
- 1/8 tsp nutmeg
- 1 tbsp butter, melted
- 2 tbsp carrots, shredded

- 1/4 tsp baking powder
- 1/4 cup milk

Toppings

- Whipped cream
- Chopped pecans
- Shredded carrots

INSTRUCTIONS

I. In a small bowl, combine all ingredients in and stir until there are no lumps.
II. Transfer batter to a microwave-safe mug.
III. Microwave for 1-1.5 minutes or until cooked through and the batter is no longer wet.
IV. Top with toppings and serve.

EASY MICROWAVE CAULIFLOWER RICE RECIPE

INGREDIENTS:

- 1 medium head cauliflower
- 3 large eggs beaten
- 2 cups mixed vegetables fresh or frozen
- salt and pepper to taste

- 1/2 teaspoon Asian sesame oil optional
- chopped green onion optional

INSTRUCTIONS

I. Wash the cauliflower with cold water and use paper towels to dry it. Remove all greens.

II. If using a box grater, cut the cauliflower into large chunks and use the medium-sized holes to grate it into pieces the size of rice. If using a food processor, cut the florets into 2-3 inch pieces, and grate the cauliflower.

III. Transfer the rice to a large paper towel or kitchen towel, squeezing to remove any excess moisture. This process will prevent your rice from becoming soggy when cooked.

IV. In a large microwave-safe bowl, add cauliflower rice, diced carrots, and peas. Cover with a lid or plastic wrap and cook on high for 2 minutes.

V. Beat the eggs in another bowl, and add it on top of the cauliflower rice. (Don't mix at this point.)

VI.   Cover with the lid or plastic wrap, and microwave on high for 45 seconds (the eggs will be half-cooked at this point).

VII.   Mix the egg with the cauliflower rice and other vegetables. Microwave for another 45-60 seconds until eggs are fully cooked.

VIII.   Season with salt, pepper, and optional sesame oil. Mix well.

IX.   Sprinkle with chopped green onions. Serve and enjoy!

MICROWAVE RAMEN RECIPE

INGREDIENTS:

- 1 package ramen noodles including flavor packets etc.
- salt-free chicken broth or cold water

Optional Additions

- green onions minced
- 1 hard boiled egg
- vegetables such as sliced carrots, mushrooms,
- meat such as leftover cooked chicken or pork

INSTRUCTIONS

I. Open the package of ramen noodles and place into a microwave safe bowl.
II. Add the flavor packet included if desired and discard the packaging.
III. Pour in water/broth to cover.
IV. Add any optional additions as desired (except for green onions, which go in at the end).
V. Microwave the ramen noodles for 1 minute on full power, followed by 30 second intervals, until steaming hot. (times may vary by microwave strength, so add extra time for tabletop microwaves, and reduce time for powerful microwaves.)
VI. Using oven mitts to prevent burns, carefully remove the hot ramen from the microwave.
VII. Garnish with optional green onions. Serve with a large spoon and chopsticks.

HEALTHY EGGS BENE-CHICK MUG

INGREDIENTS:

- 1/2 tbsp. fat-free mayonnaise

- 1/2 tsp. Best Foods/Hellmann's Dijonnaise or creamy Dijon mustard
- 1/2 tsp. lemon yogurt (or plain yogurt with a drop of lemon juice)
- 1/2 tsp. light whipped butter or light buttery spread (like Brummel & Brown), melted
- 1/2 cup fat-free liquid egg substitute (like Egg Beaters Original)
- 1 oz. (about 2 slices) 97 - 98% fat-free ham, roughly chopped
- Half a light English muffin, lightly toasted

INSTRUCTIONS

I. To make sauce, combine mayo, Dijonnaise, yogurt, and butter in a small dish. (Use a microwave-safe dish if you'd like to warm your sauce before serving.) Mix well and set aside.

II. Lightly spray a large microwave-safe mug with nonstick spray. Add egg substitute and microwave for 1 minute.

III. Gently stir and add ham. Break muffin half into bite-sized pieces and add to the mug. Microwave for 45 - 60 seconds, until set.

IV. If you like, warm sauce in the microwave, about 10 seconds. Top your egg mug with sauce, give it a little stir, and dig in!

MORNING WAFFLE DIP

INGREDIENTS:

- 1 slice center-cut bacon or turkey bacon
- 1/2 cup (about 4 large) egg whites or fat-free liquid egg substitute
- 2 frozen waffles with 3g fat or less each
- 1 slice reduced-fat cheddar cheese
- 1/4 cup sugar-free pancake syrup
- Optional seasonings: salt, black pepper, garlic powder, onion powder

INSTRUCTIONS

I. Cook bacon in a skillet sprayed with nonstick spray or on a microwave-safe plate in the microwave. (See package for temp and time.) Break in half.
II. Spray a medium microwave-safe bowl with nonstick spray. Add egg and (optional) seasonings. Microwave for 1 minute. Gently stir, and microwave for 1 more minute.

III. Toast waffles, and top one with the egg patty. Top with bacon halves, cheese, and remaining waffle.

IV. Cut in half, and serve with syrup for dipping.

KETO VANILLA MUG CAKE

INGREDIENTS:

- 1 scoop vanilla protein powder 32-34 grams
- 1/2 teaspoon baking powder
- 1 tablespoon coconut flour
- 1 tablespoon granulated sweetener of choice*
- 1 large egg
- 1/4 cup milk of choice
- 1/4 teaspoon vanilla extract
- 1 teaspoon chocolate chips of choice optional

INSTRUCTIONS

I. Grease a microwave safe bowl with cooking spray and add the protein powder, baking powder, coconut flour, sweetener of choice and mix well.

II. Add the egg and mix into the dry mixture. Add the milk of choice and vanilla extract- If the batter is too crumbly, continue adding milk of choice until a very thick batter is formed.

III. Top with chocolate chips and microwave for 60 seconds, or until just cooked in the centre.

HEALTHY ROASTED VEGGIE EGG MUFFINS

INGREDIENTS:

- 1 cup chopped bell pepper
- 1 cup chopped onion
- 1 cup chopped zucchini
- 1/4 tsp. each salt and black pepper
- 2 1/2 cups (about 20 large) egg whites or fat-free liquid egg substitute
- 2 tbsp. fat-free plain Greek yogurt
- 3/4 cup shredded reduced-fat cheddar cheese
- 1/4 cup chopped fresh basil

INSTRUCTIONS

I. Preheat oven to 400 degrees. Spray a large baking sheet and a 12-cup muffin pan with nonstick spray.

II. Lay bell pepper, onion, and zucchini on the baking sheet, evenly spaced. Season with salt and black pepper.

III. Bake for 10 minutes. Stir/rearrange veggies. Bake until softened and lightly browned, about 10 more minutes.

IV. Remove baking sheet from oven, and reduce heat to 350 degrees.

V. In a large bowl, whisk egg with Greek yogurt until mostly smooth. Stir in cheese, basil, and cooked veggies.

VI. Evenly distribute mixture among the cups of the muffin pan. (Cups will be full.) Bake until firm and cooked through, about 20 minutes.

VANILLA MUG CAKE

INGREDIENTS:

- ¼ cup +1 ½ teaspoons all-purpose flour
- 2 tablespoons sugar
- 1/4 teaspoon baking powder
- dash salt
- 2 tablespoon butter, melted
- 3 tablespoon milk
- 1/2 teaspoon vanilla extract
- 1 teaspoon sprinkles

INSTRUCTIONS

I.   Add flour, sugar, baking powder, and salt to a mug and stir together.

II. Stir in milk, melted butter, and vanilla extract until smooth, being sure to scrape the bottom of the mug. Stir in sprinkles.

III. Cook in microwave for 70-90 seconds* (until cake is just set, but still barely shiny on top). Allow to rest in microwave for 1 minute before consuming.

MICROWAVE FRENCH TOAST IN A MUG

INGREDIENTS:

- 1 tsp butter
- 3 tbsp milk
- 1 egg
- 1 tsp syrup
- 1/4 tsp vanilla extract
- 1/4 tsp cinnamon
- 1 heaping cup bread pieces

INSTRUCTIONS

I. Place the butter in a large mug or small bowl; microwave until melted (about 20 seconds).

II. Add the egg, milk, syrup, vanilla extract, and cinnamon. Whisk with a fork until well blended.

III. Add the bread pieces and gently stir making sure the egg mixture is coated evenly throughout.

IV. Microwave for 90 seconds and then check for doneness. Microwave in 20 second intervals after that for 1-2 minutes.

EASY MICROWAVE OMELETTE

INGREDIENTS:

- 2 large eggs
- Salt and pepper to taste
- 1 tablespoon milk
- 2 tablespoons cheese
- 2 tablespoons to 1/4 cup additional toppings such as diced ham diced peppers, diced onion, or bacon

INSTRUCTIONS

I.   Lightly mist a microwave safe bowl with cooking spray.

II.   Crack both eggs into the bowl. Season with salt and pepper. Whisk in the milk until the eggs are blended.

III. Sprinkle with toppings.

IV.   Microwave for 30 seconds. Remove from the microwave and stir.

V.   Microwave for an additional 30 seconds. Mix the egg mixture and repeat until the eggs are fully cooked.

OATMEAL WITH EGG

INGREDIENTS:

- 1/3 cup rolled oats
- 1/2 cup milk
- 1 egg white or egg
- 1/4 cup chopped fruit (optional)
- optional toppings: cinnamon, nut butter, seeds, chocolate chips

INSTRUCTIONS

I. Combine oats, milk, egg/egg white and fruit (if using) in a bowl and mix well.
II. Microwave for 45 seconds.
III. Stir well.
IV. Microwave another 30-60 seconds.
V. Top as desired and serve warm.

MICROWAVE HUEVOS RANCHEROS BREAKFAST BOWLS

INGREDIENTS:

- 1 whole wheat torrtilla
- 2 eggs
- 1 tbsp tomato salsa

- 1 tbsp shredded Monterey jack cheese
- 1 pinch pepper
- 1 pinch salt

INSTRUCTIONS

I.   Line the mug or bowl with the tortilla.
II. Crack the eggs into a small mixing bowl and whisk well. Add a pinch of salt and pepper. Pour egg mixture into the mug or bowl with the tortilla.
III. Top with salsa and cheese and microwave on high for 1 to 2 minutes, until the eggs puff up and are cooked through.
IV. Allow it to cool for 1-2 minutes before serving, this dish gets very hot.

PERFECT MICROWAVE PORRIDGE

INGREDIENTS:

- 1/2 cup rolled oats
- 1/2 cup water
- 1/2 cup low-fat milk

INSTRUCTIONS

I. Mix rolled oats, water, and milk in a bowl (use a large bowl to prevent spilling over when cooking).

II. Cook uncovered in the microwave on high power for 1 ½ minutes. Stir.

III. Cook for another minute. Repeat if necessary until it boils and thickens, and becomes smooth and creamy.

IV. Add your favourite toppings such as sliced banana, sultanas, canned or fresh fruit, chopped dates, or yoghurt.

BREAKFAST IN A MUG

INGREDIENTS:

- 4 Eggs
- 1/3 cup Ham, cooked and diced
- 4 Tbsp Cheddar cheese, shredded
- 2 Tbsp Milk
- 2 Green onions, sliced
- Pinch Salt

INSTRUCTIONS

I.   Cook Microwave Ready Little Potatoes according to package directions. Stir in seasoning and allow to cool slightly.

II. Chop up six Little potatoes and separate between two lightly greased mugs (around 14 to 16 oz).

III. Whisk eggs slightly and split between mugs, along with ham, cheese, milk, onion, and salt.

IV. Microwave separately on high in 40 second intervals, stirring the first two times (while there is still uncooked egg in the mug) until eggs are completely set.

V.   Serve!

MICROWAVE HAM, MUSHROOM & SWISS COFFEE CUP SCRAMBLE

INGREDIENTS:

- 1 large EGG
- 1/4 cup chopped mushrooms
- 1 thin slice deli ham, chopped (1 oz.)
- 2 Tbsp. shredded Swiss cheese

INSTRUCTIONS

I.   COAT 12-oz. microwave-safe coffee mug with cooking spray. ADD egg, water, mushrooms and ham; BEAT until blended. MICROWAVE on HIGH 30 seconds; STIR. MICROWAVE until egg is almost set, 30 to 45 seconds longer.

II. SEASON with salt and pepper if desired. TOP with cheese. SERVE immediately.

PANCAKE MUG CAKE

INGREDIENTS:

- 1/4 cup Bisquick
- 1 oz fat free milk 1/8 cup

INSTRUCTIONS

I.   In a microwave safe mug or ramekin, whisk Bisquick and milk with a small whisk for a few seconds. It's okay if small lumps remain. Heat in microwave for about 1 minute. Let pancake cool slightly before scooping out of mug and serving with syrup.

Printed in Great Britain
by Amazon

20399692R00047